EMBRACING INTERFAITH COOPERATION

Eboo Patel
on Coming Together to Change the World

A 5-SESSION STUDY BY EBOO PATEL WITH TIM SCORER

Morehouse Education Resources,
a division of Church Publishing Incorporated
Editorial Offices: 600 Grant Street, Suite 630, Denver, CO 80203

For catalogs and orders call:
1-800-672-1789
www.MorehouseEducation.org

Photos on pages 10, 28, 44, 58 and 74 courtesy of istockphotography.com. Used by permission.

Cover photo by Chris Popio © Copyright 2012 by Interfaith Youth Core. All rights reserved.

ISBN-13: 978-1-60674-119-1

TABLE OF CONTENTS

Quick Guide to the Handbook. 4

Beyond the "Quick Guide". 5

Pointers on Facilitation 9

Session 1: Interfaith Cooperation in American History. 11

Session 2: Interfaith Literacy. 29

Session 3: The Science of Interfaith Cooperation 45

Session 4: The Art of Interfaith Leadership 59

Session 5: The Role of Colleges, Seminaries, and Houses of Worship 75

QUICK GUIDE TO THIS HANDBOOK

TEN things to know as you begin to work with this resource:

1. HANDBOOK + WORKBOOK

This handbook is a guide to the group process as well as a workbook for everyone in the group.

2. A FIVE-SESSION RESOURCE

Each of the five sessions presents a distinct topic for focused group study and conversation.

3. A RESOURCE FOR MULTI-RELIGIOUS COMMUNITY

The value of this resource would be fully realized if the group using it was to be comprised of people of many faith traditions just like the one in the DVD presentation.

4. DVD-BASED RESOURCE

The teaching content in each session comes in the form of input by Eboo Patel and response by members of a small group on a DVD recording with segments of just over 30 minutes in length.

5. EVERYONE GETS EVERYTHING

This handbook addresses everyone in the group, not one group leader. There is no separate "Leader's Guide."

6. GROUP FACILITATION

The creators of this resource assume that someone will be designated as group facilitator for each session. You may choose the same person or a different person for each of the five sessions.

7. TIME FLEXIBILITY

Each of the five sessions is flexible and can be between one hour and two or more hours in length: however, if you intend to cover all the material presented, you will need the full two hours.

8. BUILD YOUR OWN SESSION

Prior to the session it is advisable for one or more members of the group to determine what to include in the group meeting time. In some cases the session outline presents options from which you can choose. In other cases the material is organized as a progression through the three or four main topics presented by Eboo Patel.

9. WITHIN EACH TOPIC IN A SESSION

Each segment in a session features a mix of input from Eboo Patel and the other members of the small group in the video, plus questions for discussion or other creative activities to guide individual and group reflection.

10. BEFORE THE SESSION, CLOSING THE SESSION AND AFTER THE SESSION

Each session opens with five activities for participants to consider as preparation for the session, closes with a blessing from one of the faith traditions that is named in the video conversation, and ends with one reflective activity as a suggestion for ongoing engagement with the topic of the session.

BEYOND THE "QUICK GUIDE"

Helpful information and guidance for anyone using this resource:

1. HANDBOOK + WORKBOOK

This handbook is a guide to the group process as well as a workbook for everyone in the group.

- We hope the handbook gives you all the information you need to feel confident in shaping the program to work for you and your fellow group members.
- The workspace provided in the handbook encourages you...
  — to respond to leading questions.
  — to write or draw your own reflections.
  — to note the helpful responses of other group members.

2. FIVE-SESSION RESOURCE

This resource presents Eboo Patel's insights on Interfaith Cooperation framed as five distinct topics of study:

1. Interfaith Cooperation in American History
2. Interfaith Literacy
3. The Science of Interfaith Cooperation
4. The Art of Interfaith Leadership
5. The Role of Colleges, Seminaries and Houses of Worship

3. A RESOURCE FOR MULTI-RELIGIOUS COMMUNITY

The value of this resource would be fully realized if the group using it was to be comprised of people of many faith traditions just like the one in the DVD presentation.

In creating this small group study resource, we set out to model a process of learning in the context of a truly multi-faith group. As you watch the DVD presentation you will meet a group that is comprised of a Jew, two Muslims, a spiritual seeker with Jain and Hindu roots, two Episcopal Christians and one Evangelical Christian who is working in the Lutheran Church.

Our challenge to you is to create your own group of religious diversity so that this study experience becomes much more than a group of Christians talking about interfaith possibilities:

- We want you to go beyond talking about something to actually experiencing it.
- We hope that you might be able to recruit a study group comprised of people from a wide variety of religious traditions and narratives.
- This study will mean so much more to you if you are able to bring together a group that is at least 50% non-Christian.

We recognize that for some of you even the task of reaching out and finding people of other faiths to participate in this study will be a new challenge and major learning experience, so here are some ways that you might begin to go about that:

- Seek out your local multi-faith or interfaith society/organization and introduce this study opportunity, inviting member organizations to advertise the program in their own faith communities.
- Contact your nearest seminary or theological school and ask to speak with the faculty member who has the most to do with

interfaith collaboration. Seek guidance from that person as to ways to go about making contact with the kind of people in other faith traditions who are ready for an experience of interfaith exploration.

- Because Eboo Patel is a prominent leader amongst American Muslims as well as in the American interfaith community, there is a special opportunity to reach out to Muslims in your community and inform them of this learning project and of your interest in involving local Muslims in the life of the learning group. You might even approach the leader of a mosque with the possibility of co-sponsoring the program, holding some sessions in your church and some in their mosque.
- Contact one of the synagogues close to you—you may already know of one that is particularly sympathetic to Jewish-Christian dialogue—and ask the rabbi if it would be possible to promote this learning opportunity in their community. Ideally, the rabbi would help you in the process of presenting the opportunity to members of the synagogue.
- Contact local media—a newspaper, a radio station, TV channel—and ask to talk about this program, using the opportunity to issue an invitation to people of other faith traditions to contact you if they are interested in knowing more about it.
- Use electronic media as well. That's how you will reach a younger demographic. Ask media-savvy people in your congregation about the best ways to go about Facebook, Twitter and YouTube outreach.

Remember: this program is more than an opportunity to talk about interfaith cooperation; it's an invitation to live it!

If You Are a Group of Diverse Religious Background...

Included in each session is a box just like this one where there are reflective questions for use by groups of mixed-faith background. These questions provide conversational openings into deepening relationship for people of different religions.

---

4. DVD-BASED RESOURCE

The teaching content in each session comes in the form of input by Eboo Patel and response by members of a small group, just over 30 minutes in length.

Eboo Patel's focused presentations and accessible academic authority stimulates thoughtful and heartfelt conversation among his listeners.

The edited conversations present group sharing that builds on Patel's initial teaching. They are intended to present to you a model of small group interaction that is personal, respectful and engaged.

You will notice that the participants in the DVD group also become our teachers. In many cases, quotes from the group members enrich the teaching component of this resource. This will also happen in your group—you will become teachers for one another.

We hope that the DVD presentations spark conversations about those things that matter most to those who are advancing the enterprise of interfaith cooperation in the 21st Century.

5. EVERYONE GETS EVERYTHING

The handbook addresses everyone in the group, not one group leader. There is no separate "Leader's Guide."

Unlike many small-group resources, this one makes no distinction between material for the group facilitator and for the participants. Everyone has it all! We believe this empowers you and your fellow group members to share creatively in the leadership.

6. GROUP FACILITATION

We designed this for you to designate a group facilitator for each session. It does not have to be the same person for all five sessions, because everyone has all the material. It is, however, essential that you and the other group members are clear about who is facilitating each session. One or two people still have to be responsible for these kinds of things:

- making arrangements for the meeting space (see notes on Meeting Space, p. 9)
- setting up the space to be conducive to conversations in a diverse small group community
- creating and leading an opening to the session (see notes on Opening, p. 9)
- helping the group decide on which elements of the guide to focus on in that session
- facilitating the group conversation for that session
- keeping track of the time
- calling the group members to attend to the standards established for the group life (see notes on Group Standards, p. 9)
- creating space in the conversation for all to participate
- keeping the conversation moving along so that the group covers all that it set out to do

- ensuring that time is taken for a satisfying closing to the session
- making sure that everyone is clear about date, location and focus for the next session
- following up with people who missed the session

7. TIME FLEXIBILITY

Each of the five sessions is flexible and can be between one hour and two or more hours in length: however, if you intend to cover all the material presented, you will need the full two hours.

We designed this resource for your group to tailor it to fit the space available in the life of the congregation or community using it. That might be Sunday morning for an hour before or after worship, two hours on a weekday evening, or 90 minutes on a weekday morning.

Some groups might decide to spend two sessions on one of the five major topics. There's enough material in each of the five outlines to do that. Rushing to get through more than the time comfortably allows results in people not having the opportunity to speak about the things that matter to them.

8. BUILD YOUR OWN SESSION

Prior to the session, it is advisable for one or more members of the group to determine what to include in the group meeting time. In some cases the session outline presents options from which you can choose. In other cases the material is organized as a progression through the three or four main topics presented by Eboo Patel.

- One or two people might take on the responsibility of shaping the session based on what they think will appeal to the group members. This responsibility could be shared from week to week.
- The group might take time at the end of one session to look ahead and decide on what they will cover in the next session. In the interest of time, it might be best to assign this planning to a couple of members of the group.
- You might decide to do your personal preparation for the session (the five activities in "Before the Session"), and when everyone comes together for the session, proceed on the basis of what topics interested people the most.

9. WITHIN EACH TOPIC IN A SESSION

Each segment in a session features a mix of input from Eboo Patel and the other members of the small group in the video, plus questions for discussion or other creative activities to guide individual and group reflection.

You will recognize that the activities and topics in the study guide emerge both from the structured teaching of Eboo Patel as well as the informal and spontaneous conversation of the group members. This parallels the process of your group, which will be initially led by the content of the DVD and the study guide, but then branch off in directions that emerge spontaneously from the particular life of your group.

10. BEFORE THE SESSION, CLOSING THE SESSION, AND AFTER THE SESSION

Each session opens with five activities for participants to consider as preparation for the session, closes with a blessing from one of the faith traditions that is named in the video conversation and ends with one reflective activity as a suggestion for ongoing engagement with the topic of the session.

- Each session opens with five activities for participants to consider as preparation for the session. We intend these activities to open in you some aspect of the topic being considered in the upcoming session. This may lead you to feel more confident when addressing the issue in the group.
- Each session has a final reflective option for participants to take from the session and use as an extension of their learning. These offer a disciplined way for each participant to continue to harvest the riches of the group conversation.
- Each session closes with a blessing from a faith tradition: Sikh, Hindu, Buddhist, Jewish and Christian, and Muslim. Another aspect of closing is *evaluation*. This is not included in an intentional way in the design of the sessions; however, evaluation is such a natural and satisfying thing to do that it could be included as part of the discipline of closing each session. It's as simple as taking time to respond to these questions:
    — What insights am I taking from this session?
    — What contributed to my learning?
    — What will I do differently as a result of my being here today?

POINTERS ON FACILITATION

1. MEETING SPACE

- Take time to prepare the space for the group. When people come into a space that has been prepared for them, they trust the hospitality, resulting in a willingness to bring the fullness of them into the conversation. Something as simple as playing recorded music as people arrive will contribute to this sense of "a space prepared for you."
- Think about how the space will encourage a spirit of reverence, intimacy and care. Will there be a table in the center of the circle where a candle can be lit each time the group meets? Is there room for other symbols that emerge from the group's life?

2. OPENING

- In the opening session, take time to go around the circle and introduce yourselves in some way.
- Every time a group comes together again, it takes each member time to feel fully included. Some take longer than others. An important function of facilitation is to help this happen with ease, so people find themselves participating fully in the conversation as soon as possible. We designed these sessions with this in mind. Encouraging people to share in the activity proposed under *Group Life* is one way of supporting that feeling of inclusion.
- The ritual of opening might include the lighting of a candle, an opening prayer, the singing of a hymn where appropriate, and the naming of each person present.

3. GROUP STANDARDS

- There are basic standards in the life of a group that are helpful to name when a new group begins. Once they are named, you can always come back to them as a point of reference if necessary. Here are two basics:
  — Everything that is said in this group remains in the group. *(confidentiality)*
  — We will begin and end at the time agreed. *(punctuality)*
- Are there any others that you need to name as you begin? Sometimes standards emerge from the life of the group and need to be named when they become evident, otherwise they are just assumed.

We the People

Article 1

SESSION | 1

INTERFAITH COOPERATION IN AMERICAN HISTORY

BEFORE THE SESSION

Many participants like to come to the group conversation after considering individually some of the issues that will be raised. The following five reflective activities are intended to open your minds, memories and emotions regarding some aspects of this session's topic. Use the space provided here to note your reflections.

1. Turn to the part of Session 1 entitled *Essential: A Founding Dream* (pp. 14-15) and read the 10 statements that are taken from Eboo Patel's opening presentation, which you will hear in the first group session. Reflect on those, knowing that they are the foundation from which Eboo lives, teaches and acts.

2. Be attentive to the news as presented in various media this week, watching for places where interfaith relationships are featured. To what extent does what you are noticing match Eboo's 10 opening statements?

3. Ask people in your family about the stories they carry concerning the way people have lived out the fundamental right of all Americans to be free to practice their own religion without fear of prejudice and bigotry.

4. Write down a list of the kind of things you celebrate that are evidence of the cultural and religious diversity of the United States, paying particular attention to what you notice in your own community.

5. What questions would you love to ask people of other faiths?

The theme of this series is *Embracing Interfaith Cooperation*. You have come together as a group, ready to uncover some responses to this question: What does interfaith cooperation look like for us as a people of faith in this second decade of the 21st Century?

This is a new group, meeting for the first time. It may be that there are people of diverse religious traditions in the group. Take a few minutes to introduce yourselves in two ways:
• by telling your name
• by introducing yourself in the context of the religious tradition(s) that is/are part of your life

In August of 2012, another group met in Chicago to learn with Eboo Patel and to grapple with the same issues that are on your agenda for these five sessions. They will introduce themselves in the same way that you have just done.

Play the first section of the DVD for Session 1, up until Eboo begins to make his presentation.

Moving from left to right they are Caryn Fields, Maham Khan, Ian Hallas, Nick Price, Gautam Srikishan and Vicki Garvey.

Play the second section of the DVD for Session 1, through Eboo's talk (about the next 12 minutes).

Eboo takes 12 minutes to paint an appealing picture of the way he sees the history and identity of the United States as a country founded in the values of a deep respect for religious diversity. He is clear, articulate and specific about his vision of the way things have been and the way they are.

Here are 10 statements that he makes during his presentation. The 10 together add up to the promise that Eboo sees in the American dream of pluralism. Go around the circle of your group and have people take turns in reading them aloud. As you do this, notice:
• when you are surprised by something new
• when you are inspired or moved
• when you have questions or wonderings

1. America is an immigrant nation. People from all over the world have come to the United States and established their families, their businesses and their cultural practices. That's how America was built.

2. You can have a big dream in America either for the kind of person you want to be, the kind of business you want to build, the kind of cultural practice or artistic endeavor you want to establish.

3. You can come to the United States and you can have freedom of conscience. You can establish your places of worship. You can pray the way you feel called by God or your consciousness.

4. Interfaith cooperation is also at the heart of the American tradition. People of diverse religious background have established themselves here in equal dignity and mutual loyalty—that is, religious pluralism.

5. People of diverse religious background who come to the United States get to continue to be followers of their religion at the same time as they are American. That hyphen between Jewish and American isn't a barrier; it's a bridge. What makes you a better Jew also makes you a better American.

6. For centuries political philosophers believed that the only way you could have diversity in a society was under dictatorship or empire. If you had a democracy, a place where people participated in civic life and where people voted for their leaders, everybody had to have the same religious identity. The exception was the United States. We are the first nation to embrace this notion that people from the four corners of the earth could come together and build a country. That was in the late 18th century. We are now looking at a world where many nations do this.

7. If you look back through American history you see multiple times along the course of the last two centuries when heroes have lived out this American tradition of religious pluralism.

8. That's the genius of the beginning of the United States. Now, as societies around the world are becoming more diverse, it has to be the genius of those societies as well. They have wonderful stories too. As they have become more diverse, these societies have realized that they too have to be countries in which interfaith cooperation is considered part of the waters of their tradition.

9. In 1893 here in Chicago, the Parliament of World Religions welcomed Buddhist, Muslim, Hindu and Catholic leaders to its podium. They declared that from now on the great religions of the world would make war no more on each other, but on the great ills that afflict humankind.

10. After Martin Luther King had gone to India and experienced the religious diversity of that country in 1959, he came back to his pulpit in Montgomery and preached on Palm Sunday: "O God, we thank You for the fact that You have inspired men and women in all nations and in all cultures. We call You different names: some call You *Allah*; some call You *Elohim*; some call You *Jehovah*; some call You *Brahma*; and come call You the *Unmoved Mover*." Let us take that heritage of interfaith cooperation, recognize that it is a key story of the American tradition, and commit ourselves to writing the next chapter in it.

Get together with one or two other people and share your responses to what you read together. Listen carefully to the response of each person, noting that even in these responses there can be a place for diversity and for respect of difference.

OPTIONS FOR FURTHER EXPLORATION

Before going on to choose from the following options for conversation and reflection, watch the rest of the DVD for Session 1, in which Eboo engages with a small interfaith group in Chicago.

OPTION 1: LIFTING UP THE STORIES

In the conversation that follows his teaching, Eboo Patel acknowledges this reality:

> *In every era there are forces of prejudice in the United States. In every era across our history the forces of pluralism, the forces that say we will be a nation where people of different backgrounds live in equal dignity and mutual loyalty, have risen up and confronted and defeated the forces of prejudice.*

Nick notes that in school the narrative that he often heard was the narrative of conflict in religious communities that could not get along. He asks, "What needs to shift?"

Eboo responds:

> *When it comes to the way we are taught about religion in typical schools in the U.S., it's one of two things:*
> - *a narrative of freedom of religion based on constitutional values and guarantees which is supported by the American legal tradition;*
> - *a narrative of religion as conflict in which people will say that different religions have always fought and will always fight.*

> *The single most important thing we can do is to say that the story of inevitable conflict between people of different religions is simply wrong. It's not inevitable. There are just as many stories of interfaith cooperation as there are of interfaith conflict. We need to lift up those stories!*

Maham takes the cue from Eboo and offers one of those stories:

> *My dad's a businessman who suffered for about 18 months when he found out that he was on some kind of a scrutiny list. It was a conversation that would take over our dinner table every night. As the American who was born and raised here, I would say, "You need to fight this in court. We have rights. This is such a denial of the American tradition!"*

> *However, my dad so believed in the American dream that he would say, "Let them do all the checking they want to do because maybe through this they will realize that I'm just as American as they are: that I'm contributing to the economy, that I'm a good businessman, that I follow ethical business practices, and that I employ several people.*

It had never struck me that way. We're always so quick to jump to perpetuate the conflict or to solve the conflict. I think conflict can be an opportunity to defend or to discuss what it is that's really bothering us. If we take a look at that context of history and conflict we face today, there's this big gap in which there's a conversation that isn't being had. That's what it points to. We've taken it so much for granted living in this country. Yes, we're a nation of freedom of religion, but how is that manifesting itself actually?

Take time to tell some of your stories that illustrate the ways that people you know are extending, through the specific actions and choices, the narrative of freedom of religion and diversity.

OPTION 2: TO BIGOTRY, NO SANCTION

In his book, *Sacred Ground: Pluralism, Prejudice, and the Promise of America*, (Boston, MA: Beacon Press, 2012), Eboo Patel expands further on the leadership of President George Washington in setting a clear standard of religious freedom right from the beginning of the founding of the United States. The following is taken from pages 14 and 15 of that book:

> In 1790, President Washington heard a plea from Moses Seixas, of the Hebrew Congregation of Newport, Rhode Island. Seixas was worried about the fate of Jews in the new nation. Would they be harassed and hated as they had been for so many centuries in Europe? Washington knew other religious communities had similar concerns. He chose the occasion of his response to Seixas to state plainly his vision for America:
>
>> The Government of the United States…gives to bigotry no sanction, to persecution no assistance, requires only that they who live under its protection should demean themselves as good citizens… May the children of the stock of Abraham who dwell in this land continue to merit and enjoy the good will of the other inhabitants—while every one shall sit in safety under his own vine and fig tree and there shall be none to make him afraid. *(George Washington, "To Bigotry No Sanction," American Treasures, Library of Congress, August 17, 1790, http://www.loc.gov/.)*

Washington is offering a vision of a national community, not simply articulating a legal doctrine: in America, people will have their identities respected, their freedoms protected, and their safety secured. They will be encouraged to cultivate good relationships with fellow Americans from other backgrounds, no matter the tensions and conflicts in the lands from which they came. And they will be invited—and expected—to contribute to the common good of their country. *Respect, relationship,* and *commitment to the common good—* those were Washington's three pillars of pluralism in a diverse democracy.

Washington came to his views through both principle and practical experience. As the leader of the Continental Army, the first truly national institution, Washington recognized he was going to need the contributions of all willing groups in America. The rampant anti-Catholic bigotry at that time was disrespectful to Catholic identity, a divisive force within the Continental Army, and a threat to the success of the American Revolution. Washington banned insults to Catholics like burning effigies of the pope, told his officers to make sure the contributions of Catholics were welcomed, and scolded those who disobeyed with words like these:

"At such a juncture, and in such circumstances, to be insulting their Religion, is so monstrous, as not to be suffered or excused" (Steven Waldman, *Founding Faith: Providence, Politics, and the Birth of Religious Freedom in American,* New York: Random House, 2009, 65).

It was the same in Washington's private life. When seeking a carpenter and a bricklayer for his Mount Vernon estate, he remarked, "If they are good workmen, they may be of Asia, Africa, or Europe. They may be Mohometans, Jews or Christians of any Sect, or they may be atheists" (Paul F. Boller, *George Washington and Religion*, (Dallas: Southern Methodist University, 1963, p. 120). What mattered is what they could build.

You will hear Eboo making reference to the same kind of principled leadership of other founding leaders: Benjamin Franklin, Thomas Jefferson and James Madison.

Discuss the following questions in your group. (**Note:** If there are more than 10 people in total, you might want to begin by discussing these questions in smaller groups of 4-5 members each. In the early sessions of a series, people are sometimes reluctant to express their views in a larger group. Breaking up into smaller configurations can really help people to feel more at ease in the conversation.)

1. How do his references to "the heroes of diversity" in American history influence the way you see the history of the United States?

2. Which other leaders, either national or regional, have made a difference in the development of the United States as a nation of religious pluralism?

3. Where do you see a need for visionary and assertive leadership to address current situations where the full practice of religious pluralism is still not realized?

OPTION 3: HOW FLAT THAT WOULD BE!

Vicky introduces a slightly different aspect of this matter of diversity and pluralism, namely the beauty of diversity. Here's what she says:

> Many of us think of ourselves as relatively educated people. I have studied American history and I didn't know these things about George Washington. In this season of a presidential election, we tend to hear a lot about our founding Christian principles: "We are a Christian nation!" No we're not! And the more we allow that rhetoric without challenge the more difficult it is for us to learn from each other, to rest on one another's strengths instead of all assuming we're all like Ian and me—Christian—a majority. How flat would that be, even though I love my Christianity! How flat would that be if that were all we were!

It's one thing to be an advocate for the dream of pluralism and freedom from prejudice, but it's something else to be in love with diversity and multicultural, multi-religious reality. How flat life would be if it were all one thing: one kind of tree, one kind of fruit, one kind of bird, one kind of human, one kind of religion.

1. Stand in a circle together and celebrate the diversity of life and religion in this way:
    * Go around the circle with each person naming some kind of diversity in life that they really love. Go around as many times as you have things to say!
    * Now go around the circle and name aspects of religious diversity that you appreciate. This will be harder because what you know has limitations.

    — It's all right to say things that you only dimly know about another religion (for example: "I like that Judaism has a special candlestick with seven candles." You may not know that it is called a *menorah* and that the design of it was given to Moses as described in Exodus 25:31 as a symbol of Divine Light.)
    — You might also say things about religions in general: "I love that religions have sacred spaces or sanctuaries that are specific to the narrative and sacred imagination of each religion."

2. Return to your chairs when you are done and discuss:
    * What did you notice in that process about your own capacity to celebrate religious diversity?

OPTION 4: SPEAKING ABOUT YOUR RELIGION AND YOUR WEIGHT

Read this conversation aloud in the group with group members speaking for Maham, Karen, Eboo and Nick:

Maham:

When I'm working with teenagers through programs at IYC (Interfaith Youth Core), a lot of time my parents get nervous. Or when they hear how I'm going to be involved in an interfaith thing they are afraid that I'm going to be converted or something like that. The truth is that religion just makes people uncomfortable. The question you have to ask is, "Why?"

Karen:

I lived in Thailand for a while. When we got there the Thai government tried to educate us about cultural differences and what we'd get into when we were thrown into the middle of nowhere. In the United States you don't ask about what someone weighs or their religion, but our teachers told us that those would be the first two questions that will come out of a Thai's mouth. And it was. Most of the people had never met someone from outside their community. Because I was thrown into that, it opened my eyes to what I believed. I was then an ambassador of myself instead of just being an American visitor. I think that the concern my parents had and what a lot of other parents have is about what will deepen their child's roots in what they raised them as.

Eboo:

If we don't cultivate and advance a positive public language of religion we simply forfeit the territory to people who have a poisonous public language. The fact is we live in a world and country that is awash with religion. Let us not be bathing in the waters of religious prejudice; let us be bathing in the waters of religious pluralism. If we want to do that, we have to be advancing that positive language.

Nick:

Part of me wonders if it's this culture too: we just don't talk about religion and we get nervous about it. I don't know if that's the kind of anxiety that then comes up if it's discussed in history. Why is it that we fixate on conflict as opposed to these stories?

Maham:

There's the irony—the Catch 22: we've created this America where we strive to be pluralistic and we say everyone has freedom of religion, so we don't talk about religion because we're giving people that privacy and that freedom. What that's done is close the door to conversation and perpetuated fear because they are unfamiliar, unknown and untouchable. But that doesn't stop the media from telling the stories of conflict. So you're stuck.

1. As you listened to the four of them speaking, where did their wide-ranging conversation most catch your attention or connect with your personal experience?

3. What kind of religious conversations would you most like to initiate with people of your faith and people of other faiths? Brainstorm a list of questions and topics you would like to pursue in open conversation. It may be that you already have religious diversity in the membership of your group. Use that to advantage by raising the questions you most want to ask one another and creating time to respond to them. If your group is more of a monoculture, then think of a way you could create opportunity to engage in open conversation with people of other faith traditions.

2. As you think about your own discomfort in speaking about personal things that really matter to you (like your religion and your weight), could you imagine being more assertive about engaging with others in conversations about what it means to you to be free to practice your own faith? (Let's leave weight out of it for now and focus on what can really make a difference.)

OPTION 5: WE ARE SIKHS TODAY!

These sessions just happened to be filmed three days after the shooting of worshippers at the Sikh Gudwara in Oak Creek, Wisconsin, in which six people and the gunman died. Gautam, Maham and Caryn reflect on the significance of this event, with Maham noting that some people in the media were trying to understand why the shooting happened. They surmised that the perpetrator of the crime accidentally mistook the Sikhs for Muslims.

Maham goes on:

> I was so grateful to the leader of the Sikh community who asked, "Why is that even relevant?" This would have been just as sick no matter who was killed. This was not the question to ask. Let's not take this conversation in a direction that validates this hatred toward a certain group.

Eboo then makes this observation:

> I'm reminded of a time when there was vandalism against a synagogue in Chicago. Some of my Muslim friends went to the vigil in support of the synagogue with signs that said, "We are Jews today." I feel that's the best of America coming to the support of the Sikh Gudwara saying, "We are Sikhs today." And the Sikhs in their remarkable grace saying, "We don't want to be known as "not Muslim." The distinction to be made is not between Muslim and Sikh. It's between "murderers" and the rest of us.

> One of the most inspiring threads in the American story are moments when communities who have been marginalized stand up not just for themselves but for deeper and bigger principles. They're not just saying, "I want freedom for me." They are actually saying, "I want freedom for everybody." The great African-American poet Langston Hughes encapsulates this in a beautiful line of poetry:

> > O, yes,
> > I say it plain,
> > America never was America to me,
> > And yet I swear this oath--
> > America will be!

Together imagine ways that you could, in your local situation, build relationship and express solidarity with people of other faith traditions.

IF YOU ARE A GROUP OF DIVERSE RELIGIOUS BACKGROUND...

You have a remarkable opportunity unfolding right here in this experience!

1. What new knowledge did you acquire today about another religious tradition?

2. What did you notice about how members of the group related to one another in this opening session?

3. How were these words descriptive of anything you observed or experienced yourself: *curious? hospitable? wary? surprised? open? guarded? revealing?*

4. In what ways did your attitude change as a result of today's session?

5. How might you include opportunities for deepening relationship, acquiring knowledge and changing attitudes in the upcoming sessions?

OPTION 6: PERSONAL REFLECTION

Following the session you will continue to think about issues raised both on the DVD and in your small group. This suggestion for journaling is offered to support you in continuing your reflection beyond the session time.

Write a letter to someone who is in a position to continue to maintain the powerful tradition of interfaith cooperation that is bedrock of American identity. This could be anyone from a teacher of your children or grandchildren to the President of the United States. Your intention is to support, encourage and inspire them.

From the Sikh tradition:

Ardaas*

> You are the Divine Master, to You I offer this prayer.
> This body and soul are all Your property.
> You are our Mother and Father, we are Your children.
> Within Your Grace, there are so many joys!
> No one knows Your limits,
> O highest of the high, most generous Divine.
> The whole of creation is strung on Your thread.
> That which has come from You is under Your command.
> You alone know Your state and extent.
> I Nanak, Your slave, am forever a sacrifice.

Divine Mother and Father,

(Insert personal prayers; add your own in the space provided):
- Bless these new friendships.
- Deepen our capacity to embrace differences as gift.
- Open the fullness of our lives to receive sacred insight from all traditions.
-
-
-
-
-
-
-

—Vaheguru Ji Ka Khalsa, Vaheguru Ji Ki Fateh.

Ardaas is the name of the prayer that this verse belongs to. It's a prayer of supplication.

Sikh scriptures are written in the first and second person. While various Gurus contributed to the scriptures, they each referred to themselves as *Nanak*, after the first Sikh Guru. So when Sikh scriptures are read they are read in the first and second person, as conversations between the Gurus and the Divine. Sikhs get a chance to step into the shoes of the Gurus and experience their relationship with the Divine.

The last line is the equivalent of *Amen*. Sikhs say it at the end of all their prayers. *Khalsa* refers to all spiritual beings connected to the Divine. *Vaheguru* is the Sikh word for the Divine. It means, "Wow! Amazing Deliverer from darkness to light."

So the line means *To Vaheguru belongs the Khalsa, To Vaheguru belongs all triumph*. In this line, by "triumph" Sikhs mean "all blessings and successes come from the Divine." They also use this line as a greeting between Sikhs. So when they greet each other, and when they finish their prayers, they remind themselves that they belong to the Divine, and all blessings and triumphs belong to the Divine. Everything is sourced back to the Divine.

—With appreciation to Sukhvinder Vinning, Surrey, BC, Canada,
for this insight into Sikh prayers.

SESSION | 2

INTERFAITH LITERACY

BEFORE THE SESSION

Many participants like to come to the group conversation after considering individually some of the issues that will be raised. The following five reflective activities are intended to open your minds, memories and emotions regarding some aspects of this session's topic. Use the space provided here to note your reflections.

1. As you drive around your community what signs do you see of the presence of people of other faith traditions? When you see sanctuaries and meeting places of other faiths what clues do you get about the things that matter to them? What questions would you want to ask of each one?

2. Make a cake, a garden bed, a birdhouse, a piece of music, a website, a piece of pottery, a poem, a crossword puzzle, a collage or whatever it is that you love to make and put into that thing all that you appreciate about your own faith tradition. Invite someone of another tradition to come and experience that thing and everything you put into it.

3. Draw a five-pointed star on a blank sheet of paper. At each point of the star write something you appreciate about other faith traditions or times when you have had engagement with people of other faiths that have been positive for you. In the space between each point, write one thing that you appreciate about your faith. Look for connections between the points and the valleys.

4. In what ways does your own faith tradition encourage you to make connection with people of other faiths or to learn more about those other traditions? If you're not sure how to answer that, call a priest, a theological school or an experienced member of your congregation and collect responses. Bring them to the group.

5. Write on separate pieces of paper values that are common to all faith traditions. Post them around the house in prominent places. For a month, pay attention to those, allowing yourself to think more deeply about what it means for these values to be shared across traditions.

This is the second meeting of the group. There is already a sense of membership carried over from the first session; but there's a good chance there may be people attending for the first time.

If you have been successful in creating a multi-faith group, then this time of intentional hospitality and of meeting one another is even more critical than usual. Take time to check in as you did in the first session, learning names and religious affiliations.

If it seems like a good idea to check in further, you could anticipate one of the themes of the session and ask people to tell one thing that they really appreciate about their own faith tradition.

Interfaith Literacy is the knowledge base that we need in order to be citizens and leaders in a religiously diverse society.

 Play the whole DVD presentation for Session 2

Interfaith Literacy consists of four specific areas of activity. The first is…

APPRECIATIVE KNOWLEDGE

There are two types of *Appreciative Knowledge.* The first is *something you would like others to appreciate about your tradition.*

For example, Eboo would like non-Muslims to know the most common prayer in Islam: "*Bismillah ir-Rahman ir-Raheem,*" which means "In the name of God, the Compassionate, the Merciful."

He is clear about why this is important to him:

> *Compassion and mercy are central values in Islam. These are central attributes of God and the attributes Muslims aspire to in their own lives. The prophet Muhammad was sent by God as a special mercy upon all the worlds.*

Here are some examples of this first type of appreciative knowledge that we hear on the DVD from the members of the group that met with Eboo:

Gautam:

> *In Jainism I appreciate the principle of Ahimsa (non-violence) which is very central to my belief system. It comes out of the belief that every living being has a soul and that therefore every living being should be respected.*

Vicki:

> *There's a sign in this country near most Episcopal churches, which is red, white and light blue and says, "The Episcopal Church Welcomes You." When we take that seriously we're doing very good work. We're doing the hospitality of God. We're doing it from deep within our tradition which really welcomes, questions and holds these questions lightly and wants to engage in conversations with other people, wants, in fact, to do what Jesus did which is to welcome everybody to the table. Anybody who wants to sit with anybody else—is willing to sit with anybody else at the table—is welcome among us.*

Ian:

> *In the recent context of the Episcopal Church it's largely been about LGBT (lesbian, gay, bisexual, transgendered) issues, but when we bring it to a context like this, it's what you said, Vicki, about bringing everybody to the table and having everybody there as a representative regardless of faith background, and then to just talk about who you are, what you're doing, and the good impact that you're willing and wanting to have on the world.*

Nick:

> *The incarnation and atonement of Jesus shape the understanding of Evangelical Christians about what it means to love others and are very powerful for me and my community. The incarnation is the idea that the transcendent God of the universe loves us so much that he's willing to move into the neighborhood to be one of us, to be near us and to draw us into relationship with him. That expression of God's divine love comes in Christ. The atonement is the idea that God not only loves us and moves into our neighborhood but that he's also willing to choose us over himself to the point of sacrifice on our behalf.*

Maham:

> *I wish from my tradition that people understood that there's a greater definition of Jihad than people generally know or understand. Jihad is a very active struggle within yourself to fix your own shortcomings and to better your local community. If there's a need, a social injustice, if there are homeless people, hungry people, your Jihad is to actually deal with that situation and that problem. It's so ironic that the word Jihad is thought of as what happened on 9/11 and this Muslim crusade. I wish people could understand that there's a greater Jihad that Muslims are fighting, and if we'd been fighting it better by being more involved in our communities it would have been very different with what happened after 9/11—the backlash—to understand that this is not the religion itself.*

Caryn:

> *There are words of a song I grew up with:*
>   *Al sh'loshah d'varim haolam omed:*
>   *Al haTorah, v'al ha-avodah, v'al g'milut chasadim.*
> *Which means:*
>   *The world depends on three things: on Torah, on worship and on acts of loving kindness (Pirkei Avot 1:2).*
>
> *I think that people get caught on the first two things when looking at the Jewish tradition and don't necessarily talk about or act out "acts of loving kindness." That's where I've spent a lot of my upbringing and even the career path I've chosen and the life I live day-to-day. I think that "acts of loving kindness" also relate back to the first two (Torah and worship) and something as simple as saving a life, even if you have to break other laws to do that. I think that cuts across all religious boundaries.*

Eboo:

> *What Caryn has just shared is a shared value with Islam in which there is also a line that to save a life is to have saved all of humanity.*

What is one thing you would like people of other faiths to appreciate about your religion?

The second type of *Appreciative Knowledge* is *something you admire and appreciate about another religious tradition.*

Here are two examples of this second type of appreciative knowledge from the members of the group:

Caryn:

> Thanissaro Bhikkhu explains, "The early Buddhist notion of karma focused on the liberating potential of what the mind is doing with every moment. Who you are—what you come from—is not anywhere near as important as the mind's motives for what it is doing right now." In the fast pace world that many of us get caught up in today, it is hard to live in the moment, instead we tend to look to the past as we plan for the future. What happened to the present? Although I am not Buddhist, I appreciate what karma teaches—stop, take a deep breath and live in the moment. I don't think there could be a more valuable lesson in any religion.

Vicki:

> One of the things I have long appreciated about Judaism—and my guess is that it's also represented under different names in other faith traditions—is the principle of tikkun olam *("mending the world")*, which understands that it is our responsibility to be about the work of repairing the rents in the cosmos in our corner of creation whether we find such undoings in the cares and needs of other people, the despoliation of the natural world or anywhere else. It's a principle that says that each of us is responsible and that together we can keep on being the co-creators God called us to be way back in the beginning, and bring all that is back to the

"goodness" it had when God who first spoke it and us into being.

Gautam:

> One thing I really like from the Sikh tradition is called langar. *Langar is a free, vegetarian meal provided at a Sikh gurdwara, or house of worship. It is specifically meant to serve all people regardless of religion, race, gender or other identity. Vegetarian food is served to accommodate people of different backgrounds with various dietary restrictions.*

Ian:

> One thing I appreciate about the Muslim faith is their daily prayer rituals, including, but not limited to, praying five times a day. This sort of devotion was much more prevalent in Christianity, with canonical hours, many centruies ago, but has since disappeared in mainstream Christianity. I believe that Christians would all benefit from more consistent prayer time.

What is one thing you appreciate about one or two other religions?

Interfaith Literacy is the knowledge base that we need in order to be citizens and leaders in a religiously diverse society.

Interfaith Literacy consists of four specific areas of activity. The second is…

A THEOLOGY OF INTERFAITH COOPERATION

A Theology of Interfaith Cooperation is knowing what it is from your own tradition that would inspire you to engage positively with people from other religions. Eboo states:

> *We engage in interfaith cooperation not in spite of being Muslim or Jewish or Christian or humanist, but because our texts, our heroes and the important moments in our religious civilizations inspire and command us to do that.*

Eboo illustrates from his Muslim tradition:

> *There is a line in the Qur'an (Surah 49:13):* O humankind! We created you from a single (pair) of a male and a female, and made you into nations and tribes, that ye may know each other not that ye may despise (each other).

> *In that line there is a requirement for me as a Muslim to view the diversity of the human community as enriching and to take proactive steps to get to know it.*

What is it *from your own tradition* that would inspire you to engage positively with people from other religions? That might be things like texts, heroes of the faith and theological insights.

Interfaith Literacy is the knowledge base that we need in order to be citizens and leaders in a religiously diverse society.

Interfaith Literacy consists of four specific areas of activity. The third is…

KNOWING THE STORY OF INTERFAITH COOPERATION IN HUMAN THINKING AND HERITAGE

Interfaith cooperation is an inspiring arc in the human condition! Eboo observes:

> *India was freed from British rule in part because Mahatma Gandhi, the great Hindu leader, worked together with Bacha Khan, the great Muslim leader.*

> *Martin Luther King Junior's non-violence was sparked by learning about Mahatma Gandhi as a seminary student and the advanced correspondence with Thich Nhat Hanh, the great Buddhist monk.*

In our history as human beings there is a great story of interfaith cooperation and we need to know something of that story. We need to know this history because the story of the clash of civilizations or the inevitability of religious conflict is so widespread and pervasive.

In Eboo Patel's book, *Sacred Ground: Pluralism, Prejudice and the Promise of America* (Boston, MA: Beacon Press, 2012), he tells the Dalai Lama's story about Thomas Merton's visit to his residence in Dharamsalla in 1968. This is an example of a marker event in the journey of interfaith cooperation. Here's how Eboo writes about it:

The two monks, one Buddhist, one Christian, compare their robes, their meditation practices, the relationship between ritual, values, and spirituality in their respective traditions. That personal narrative provides a doorway for the Dalai Lama to discuss Tibet's history of interfaith encounter, with a special focus on the story of an Italian Jesuit who spent enough years in dialogue with Buddhist monks that he wrote a lengthy text about the value of comparative religious study in Tibetan. The Dalai Lama picks up the thread of the meeting with Merton again in his chapter on Christianity, where he emphasizes "the centrality of the compassionate ideal of relieving others from suffering as a key motivation in both Buddhism and Christianity."* In his early brush with Christianity, the Dalai Lama had found the stark and bloody image of Jesus on the cross somewhat startling. Merton points him to the picture of the Virgin Mary cradling the Baby Jesus and the verses in the Bible that speak of love, and emphasizes to the Dalai Lama that all of Christianity—the sacrifice, the blood, the cross—has to be understood in light of that single, central value: love.

*His Holiness The Dalai Lama, *Toward a True Kinship of Faiths: How the World's Religions Can Come Together* (New York: Doubleday, 2010)

What are some of the great stories, heroes and events of interfaith cooperation that inspire you?

Interfaith Literacy is the knowledge base that we need in order to be citizens and leaders in a religiously diverse society.

Interfaith Literacy consists of four specific areas of activity. The fourth is…

KNOWING THE SHARED VALUES
BETWEEN AND ACROSS DIFFERENT RELIGIONS

When we identify shared values that are common to many traditions we create the space for the articulation of beautiful and enriching particularities within each tradition.

1. Here are four shared values that cut across all religions. Take time to listen to the members of your group speaking about times when each of these was visible as a value in their faith community or faith story:
   • Mercy
   • Compassion
   • Justice
   • Hospitality

2. What do you notice happens in your conversation across religious differences when you share from the perspective of these shared values?

Interfaith Literacy depends on genuine and respectful interaction.

As the group members engaged in their own interfaith interaction, these helpful insights emerged from their conversation. These are the ways they have found to promote interfaith literacy through interaction:

- By being free to ask questions; Ian:

    The only way I feel my education is authenticated is by asking questions. That's how I truly learn and understand. It adds an element of respect because if I can ask a personal question, the answer becomes more substantial…you have to ask your questions. You have to confront these issues that you're willing to talk about.

- By interacting in the everyday ordinary tasks of our living; Nick:

    Appreciative knowledge comes about because we're learning to interact as human beings, always trying to contextualize our faith in our life experiences. My favorite interaction with you is when we talk about our kids. How is it that you're wrestling with being a Muslim parent and passing on that faith to your children; and I'm wrestling as a Christian parent passing on that faith to my kids. All of a sudden there's room for appreciative knowledge and gaining that understanding… It goes a little deeper than saying, "You're a religious parent and I'm a religious parent; isn't that great we're religious parents!"

- By being available to shatter misinformed judgments in the media; Maham:

    Why is it so easy for you to believe that the people you are hearing about in the news are the true face of Islam and this entire landscape including this lovely woman in front of you, is not the real face of Islam? If you start to have these conversations and focus on the positive things it becomes clearer.

- By putting ourselves into the place of the person who is usually in the minority; Vicki:

    I'm a person who really likes change. This excites me a lot except when it's a little uncomfortable. Then I have to start questioning myself and what I've always assumed is correct. I think of occasions when we have the opportunity to be in the minority, to go and be the person who doesn't know, to go into another community and to ask questions and to be able to be willing to be questioned. That's the only way we do have a capacity to have these relationships which allow us to ask those kind of deeper questions. When I'm the one who is different in the group it makes me think of myself differently and it invites the other to perhaps think of themselves differently.

• By trusting our capacity to speak from our own appreciative knowledge and not need to be a religious experts; Eboo:

> *I don't think we need to be theological experts. We need to be able to tell other people some appreciative knowledge about our tradition. You can say, "Jesus was kind to people from other traditions. That's why I work with people from other backgrounds." Or you can have a really intricate exegesis of the Good Samaritan story. We don't need to be deep experts; we just need to be comfortable enough with appreciative knowledge from our own tradition and be open to asking questions of people in other traditions.*

1. Which of these particularly speak to you?

2. What other guidelines come to mind as you think about how to promote interfaith literacy through interaction?

IF YOU ARE A GROUP OF DIVERSE RELIGIOUS BACKGROUND...

There has been an enormous amount of material in this session that will have opened up opportunities for sharing knowledge and building relationship.

1. How are you being changed by having this opportunity to engage with people of other faith traditions about things that matter to all of you?

Following the session you will continue to think about issues raised both on the DVD and in your small group. This suggestion is offered to support you in continuing your reflection beyond the session time.

Did you notice in the section on "Appreciative Knowledge" how Caryn made this observation about the gift of Buddhism?

> *In the fast pace world that many of us get caught up in today, it is hard to live in the moment, instead we tend to look to the past as we plan for the future. What happened to the present? Although I am not Buddhist, I appreciate what karma teaches—stop, take a deep breath and live in the moment. I don't think there could be a more valuable lesson in any religion.*

Find time this week for meditation. If you already have experience of meditation or your own practice, just follow that. If you have no experience of meditation, set aside at least 20 minutes when you can be assured of not being interrupted. Assume a meditation position that's comfortable for you. Close your eyes. Focus on your breath, the rhythm of the in-breath (inhaling) and the out-breath (exhaling). Whenever your mind wanders return to your breath.

After this initial experience you might like to add some words to the process—words that connect to Caryn's observations about being in the present moment, for example:

Inhale:	I calm myself.
Exhale:	I smile.
Inhale:	I dwell in the present moment.
Exhale:	It is a wonderful moment.

CLOSING BLESSING

Close the session with this Buddhist blessing or aspiration prayer called the Four Immeasurables:

May all beings have happiness and the causes of happiness.
May all beings be free from suffering and the causes of suffering.
May all beings never be separated from the supreme joy beyond sorrow.
May all beings abide in equanimity, free from attachment and aversion,
Seeing the equality of all that lives.

SESSION | 3

THE SCIENCE OF INTERFAITH COOPERATION

BEFORE THE SESSION

Many participants like to come to the group conversation after considering individually some of the issues that will be raised. The following five reflective activities are intended to open your minds, memories and emotions regarding some aspects of this session's topic. Use the space provided here to note your reflections.

1. In the first section of this session you will find a 12-point questionnaire that will be part of the learning process (pp. 47-48). You might find it helpful to respond to those questions prior to the session.

2. Give yourself just 15 minutes to write as much personal information as you can in the three columns below. The intention is to encourage you to think about the place of these three key elements in your life.

KNOWLEDGE ABOUT OTHER RELIGIONS	RELATIONSHIPS WITH PEOPLE OF OTHER RELIGIONS	ATTITUDES TO PEOPLE OF OTHER RELIGIONS

3. How have your attitudes to people of other religions changed over the years? How would you describe your attitude now? Does it vary depending on what group the other belongs to? What relationships and experiences over the years have affected your attitude?

4. *Mission Possible:* Contact someone you may or may not know from another faith tradition and invite them to meet you (coffee cafe? tea at your place? walk in the park? lunch?) for a conversation that is intended to deepen knowledge, broaden relationship and change attitude.

5. When have you learned something about another tradition that changed your view of that tradition?

This is the third meeting of the group. There is now a sense of membership carried over from the first two sessions.

If you have been successful in creating a multi-faith group, then this time of intentional hospitality and of meeting one another is even more critical than usual. Take time to check in as you did in the first two sessions, being particularly attentive to celebrations, festivals and traditional observances that fall in this season.

ESSENTIAL: THE INTERFAITH TRIANGLE

There are three key elements in the *Science of Interfaith Cooperation* as presented by Eboo Patel:
• Attitudes
• Knowledge
• Relationships

Before we hear Eboo define these and speak about their interrelatedness, let's examine each one in reference to our *own* attitudes, knowledge and relationships.

INTERFAITH QUIZ

In pairs or triads respond to these twelve questions:

1. Would you vote for someone if you knew he or she was an atheist? *(Attitudes)*

2. What is the name of the sacred text of Islam? *(Knowledge)*

3. Name some of the people that you know personally from other faith traditions. *(Relationships)*

4. Do you think that it is necessary that Muslims go through additional security at airports? *(Attitudes)*

5. What are the first five books of Hebrew Scriptures? *(Knowledge)*

6. What places of worship of other religions have you visited? *(Relationships)*

7. Do you think that Mormons should serve on the Supreme Court? *(Attitudes)*

8. What is the religion in which members worship in a sacred temple known as a *gurdwara*. *(Knowledge)*

9. What are the visible signs of other religious traditions in your community (buildings, areas, signs and symbols, clothing, festivals, music, etc.)? In what ways have you engaged with that visible presence? *(Relationships)*

10. How do you view people of other religions differently than your parents did? *(Attitudes)*

11. Name as many of the seven sacraments of Catholicism as you can. *(Knowledge)*

12. When has your view of religious diversity been affected by a family member or friend entering into a relationship with someone of a different religious background? *(Relationships and Attitudes)*

Return to the whole group and share whatever you learned about yourself from taking this quiz.

Play the first section of the DVD for Session 3, through Eboo's talk (about the next 12 minutes).

THE INTERFAITH TRIANGLE

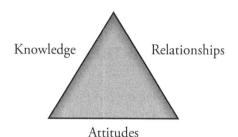

In the DVD presentation, Eboo introduces us to the three elements of the Science of Interfaith Cooperation: *attitudes, knowledge and relationships.* He speaks about the interplay between these three things in his book, *Sacred Ground: Pluralism and Prejudice and the Promise of America* (Boston, MA: Beacon Press, 2012):

> The more I studied this area, the more I started to see attitudes, knowledge, and relationships as three sides of a triangle. *If you know some (accurate and positive) things about a religion, and you know some people from that religion, you are far more likely to have positive attitudes toward that tradition and that community.* [Emphasis added.] The more favorable your attitude, the more open you will be to new relationships and additional appreciative knowledge. A couple of cycles around this triangle, and people from different faiths are starting to smile at each other on the streets instead of looking away or crossing to the other side. A few more cycles— more knowledge, more friends, more favorable attitudes—and people might start to say, "We ought to do something with those people who worship in that place called a mosque or a gurdwara down the street."

But the triangle works the other way as well. You can run reverse cycles on it. *People without much knowledge about other religions and with little contact with people from those communities are far more likely to harbor negative attitudes toward those traditions and communities.* [Emphasis added.] If movements emerge to fill those gaps in knowledge and relationships with negative information and ugly representations, people's attitudes go from negative to vociferously opposed… And that leads to community action as well—like arson attacks on mosque construction sites.

You don't need to be a professor at Harvard or Princeton to know in your gut that positive relationships with people of other faiths and appreciative knowledge of their traditions will improve people's attitudes toward religious diversity. But it's one thing to feel something in your bones and another thing to have the data that proves beyond a shadow of a doubt that it is true. The data helps convince skeptics, but perhaps even more important, it focuses the efforts of activists. Now that we know that the key leverage points in building religious pluralism are appreciative knowledge and meaningful relationships, interfaith organizations can design their programs to increase these two factors.

With reference to the two statements in italics above, discuss the ways that the dynamics of the Interfaith Triangle have been operative in your attitudes toward people of other religions.

OPTIONS FOR FURTHER EXPLORATION

Before going on to choose from the following options for conversation and reflection, watch the rest of the DVD for Session 3 in which Eboo engages with a small interfaith group in Chicago.

OPTION 1: 9/11 AND THE INTERFAITH TRIANGLE

Eboo:

The 9/11 attacks were highly deliberate in the way that so many people were able to see them. The second plane went into the building minutes after the first one. Osama bin Laden and al-Qaeda knew the camera would be on. There was not only heinous murder, there was the ugly visual imagery saying, "This is what Islam is like!" That is in recent times the best example of the availability heuristic. When you think about Islam, the first image that comes to mind is that plane going into the building.

Al-Qaeda knows the interfaith triangle! They're working it in reverse. They know that if you have an ugly representation of a Muslim in Osama bin Laden, if you have an ugly knowledge base of Islam in relation to September 11, your attitudes will plummet. We have to be better than that! We have to work the interfaith triangle in the opposite direction: the appreciative knowledge, the positive relationships.

This example of the Interfaith Triangle in action highlights the degree to which people who pay attention to what's going on in the world can be manipulated by those who will work the triangle in reverse.

Maham tells a 9/11 story about how she turned the triangle in a positive direction:

Maham:

At 9/11, I was a college student and President of the Muslim Students Association. I remember there was so much fear on campus including from the Muslims because we didn't know how to perceive all that was going on. Basically, there was a group of Muslim students who wanted to pray in the main hall to say, "We have freedom of religion; this is our right to believe." They were taking a stand because there was a lot of backlash on campus. I was really nervous about the whole event because maybe we just weren't ready for it.

So the students started to pray. There was a young boy who I remember particularly because he was very angry. I remember him standing at the top of the heads of the men who were praying prostrate with their heads touching the ground. He just stood at the head. I remember thinking, "This can't be good!" and being very nervous about what was about to happen. He just stood with this look on his face so that you knew he was really angry. The boys stopped their prayers because they knew that maybe a confrontation was about to happen. They got up and one of the Muslim boys and the angry guy were doing this kind of stare down with one another. I was thinking, "O God, this is not going as well as we thought. I don't know what to do with this." I was trying to be a leader.

Coincidentally, a week later I was asked to speak at the Intervarsity Christian Fellowship because their president was a friend of mine. She said she'd like me to come in and talk about some of the things we talk about all the time at a personal level because a lot of the kids in my group were very upset and angry. So I went to speak and in walked the angry guy. I remember thinking, "O man!" He was very angry, very closed off, and he just observed. We were talking in the group and there were a lot of questions and answers. Then there was this moment when someone asked me, "So how do you really feel about all of this?" I don't know what it was, but I began to cry. I just really had this moment when I was so frustrated because everything I've ever learned about my faith had gone out the window. I didn't understand what was happening and I didn't understand why there wasn't an understanding that an entire

faith group couldn't be behind this big 9/11 scheme. I was truly devastated. I had this moment when I was just weeping and I noticed that the angry guy softened a bit.

The following day when I went to watch the boys pray in the hall again, the angry guy was standing in front of them once again, not with his feet toward their heads, but a few yards in front of them. I was baffled and said, "What are you doing. This is strange behavior." He said, "I just wanted to make sure that these guys could pray without interruption." It was such a change in attitude! I asked him about what changed his mind. He said, "You changed my heart because you came in and I saw you in pain and my faith tradition says, 'When you see someone in pain, it's your job as a Christian to extend your hand.'"

That one relationship that we built changed him, changed me and probably averted a huge crisis on campus. One step at a time. One person at a time. One relationship at a time.

1. What are your stories of individuals working the interfaith triangle to either negative or positive ends?

3. When have you been successful in influencing people's attitudes toward positive pluralism and away from prejudice?

2. When have you felt influenced by people who have used the dynamics of the Interfaith Triangle to either positive or negative outcomes?

OPTION 2: ELSEWHERE THERE BE MONSTERS!

Listen to these two stories from Caryn and Eboo and then respond to the reflective prompts that follow:

Caryn:

I was going to be living abroad for a year and we got a list of names of those who were going. My mum suggested that we should Facebook these people. We pulled up the girl who was going to be geographically closest to where I was living. Right away stereotyping started firing off in my head. She was an adorable blonde girl with 9 siblings and young-looking parents. Instead of thinking about this nice-looking girl that I was going to be living near, and thinking that I should get to know her, all kinds of judgments started going through my head about what this would mean. I wondered what my life was going to look like for the next year given that this was likely the only girl I could speak to in my native tongue and have a relationship with.

She ended up being an amazing girl. When you look at the two of us we are completely different in our religion and upbringing, yet we were so similar in other ways that we would stay up until two in the morning when we were traveling to each other's locations. My mum didn't have that personal relationship with her because she was half way around the world. Even now in the stories I tell my mum she thinks, "O no; this is the person my daughter is spending her time with!" It taught me how readily available is the opportunity to reach out in a positive way instead of internalizing things and scaring myself. It's so easy to buy into the negative!

Eboo:

There's a famous story of a German map-maker some centuries back who created a world map and put at the center of it the continent of Europe and wrote on it: "Elsewhere there be monsters!" That's a terrific example of the principle that if you have no knowledge of something, the first knowledge you are likely to believe is prejudicial, ugly and negative.

One of the things we say at Interfaith Youth Core is that when it comes to religious diversity we are not dealing in neutral territory. It's not like if you say nothing about Jews, nothing will be said. It's more like the forces of prejudice and anti-Semitism out there will be the ones who own the territory. So right now we live in an era when the winds of religious prejudice are blowing hard and fast and the forces that want to sow division and advance prejudice are not shy. That means that those of us who know the science of interfaith cooperation, who have acquired interfaith literacy, who are inspired by the heritage of interfaith cooperation in America and beyond, have to be busy writing the next chapter.

1. When have you noticed that tendency in yourself to fall into negative judgments about an individual or group when you have scant information about them? Another way to put it: when have you put yourself at the centre of the map and drawn a line around yourself, marking off what you know from what is unknown. Beyond that you wrote: "Elsewhere there be monsters."

3. In what ways are you already writing a new chapter in the heritage of interfaith cooperation?

2. How have you successfully gone about the destruction of these monsters of the fearful imagination?

OPTION 3: MIND-CHANGING EXPERIENCES

Maham responded by talking about a time when the mosque where she was meeting for some uninspiring interfaith discussions had to go through a year of reconstruction. The neighboring Methodist church invited them to hold their Friday prayers in the basement of the Methodist church for the entire duration of the construction year. Maham said that everything else went out the window in her life: she was so moved by the welcome they received. Being there for prayers she could see their books and their congregation coming to worship. They were forced by circumstances to talk to one another. The Methodists would ask the members of Maham's community about their prayers. It was the most organic form of interfaith collaboration, cooperation and literacy she had ever experienced.

When have you learned something about another tradition that changed your view of that tradition?

IF YOU ARE A GROUP OF DIVERSE RELIGIOUS BACKGROUND...

You could design a quiz for one another, including knowledge that you think is essential for someone to know as they learn about your faith.

1. Take the opportunity to use this group as a way to test the theory of The Interfaith Triangle. How are your attitudes changing as a result of building relationships and extending knowledge? How is your change in attitude opening you to new relationships?

2. Are there things you can learn from one another about the negative side of The Interfaith Triangle? That is, have people in your group experienced negative attitudes toward their tradition and community as a result of absence of knowledge and relationship?

3. In what ways could you as a diverse group, extend knowledge, build relationship and change attitudes beyond this study group?

4. What do you like about being together?

OPTION 4: PERSONAL REFLECTION

Following the session you will continue to think about issues raised both on the DVD and in your small group. This suggestion for journaling is offered to support you in continuing your reflection beyond the session time.

Continue to use this framework as a way of bearing witness to your own growth in interfaith cooperation. Instead of columns on a page, you might have separate pages in a notebook or journal where you continue to reflect on your growth in each of these areas:

KNOWLEDGE ABOUT OTHER RELIGIONS	RELATIONSHIPS WITH PEOPLE OF OTHER RELIGIONS	ATTITUDES TO PEOPLE OF OTHER RELIGIONS

CLOSING

From Hindu tradition comes this a universal vedic prayer, a prayer for enlightenment:

Asatoma Sadgamaya
Thamaso Maa Jyotir Gamaya
Mrithyor Maa Amrutham Gamaya
Aum Shanti Shanti Shantihi

Lead me from the unreal to the real.
Lead me from darkness to light.
Lead me from death to immortality.
May there be peace everywhere.

SESSION | 4

THE ART OF INTERFAITH LEADERSHIP

BEFORE THE SESSION

Many participants like to come to the group conversation after considering individually some of the issues that will be raised. The following five reflective activities are intended to open your minds, memories and emotions regarding some aspects of this session's topic. Use the space provided here to note your reflections.

1. Martin Luther King Jr. is featured in Eboo's teaching in this session. In anticipation of that, you might choose to go online and watch some film of King's preaching. The pieces are short, but incredibly inspiring. A search online will bring you to YouTube videos like those listed here. For these or any others you may watch, record your response in the space provided:
   - www.youtube.com/watch?v=HlvEiBRgp2M&feature=fvwrel
   - www.youtube.com/watch?v=o0FiCxZKuv8
   - www.youtube.com/watch?v=130J-FdZDtY&feature=related
   - www.youtube.com/watch?v=vk1VANxSNyg&feature=related

2. Using your voice in leadership is an important part of this session. Spend this time prior to the next session noticing when you feel free to use your voice and when you feel silenced, that is, when you have something important you would like to say but don't feel free to do that because of the pressures on you—subtle and not so subtle—not to speak.

3. What are the interreligious issues that matter to you? If you are not sure how to answer that, contact some people from other traditions and ask them about the issues they are facing these days. What are the interreligious issues right in your own back yard? There are always interreligious tensions, often much closer than we know. You will become more inspired to use your voice and influence when you know more clearly what the issues are where you live, and how they are affecting people in your region or community.

4. Eboo Patel encourages us to look beyond our own leadership to the ways that we support and encourage others to exercise their own positive leadership. Take time to remember people who have encouraged you in the development of your leadership. Then think about those on whom you have had a positive influence in liberating their leadership. Be careful not to dismiss your own power in these matters.

5. Eboo Patel says, *"We have to recognize that the territory is not neutral. The winds of prejudice and conflict and tension are blowing and there are people who are building barriers and bombs of religion. If I'm not building a bridge, I just forfeit the territory to them."* Peruse your newspaper, a news magazine, online news services or a TV news channel in search of ways that people are choosing to build bridges and to take positive action so that more and more territory is colored by compassion, justice, radical acceptance and inclusiveness. It's happening. We have to notice.

This is the fourth meeting of the group. In this session we come to the matter of leadership. How have you been exercising leadership in your group? The study guide is designed to encourage shared leadership. Perhaps your group designated a facilitator right from the beginning of the program and that person has been carrying out that responsibility. Perhaps you decided to share the leadership and it has naturally moved around the group with people taking on facilitation at different times. There could be many ways that you are doing the three essential things of group life: completing the task at hand, maintaining the life of the group, and taking care of the individual members.

It's very easy for groups to sink into a pattern of leadership and not stop to ask, every once in a while, if that way is still working well for them. Take a moment and talk about how things are going in terms of the facilitation of your group process. You have two sessions left. Is there anything you want to do differently, not necessarily because it's not working, but because it would just be good for you to try something different?

Let's review the learning journey we have been on so far:

Session 1:
We began by appreciating the tradition and history of Interfaith Cooperation in America.

Session 2:
In the second session, we saw how Interfaith Literacy includes these four things:
• appreciative knowledge
• a theology of interfaith cooperation
• knowing the story of interfaith cooperation in human thinking and heritage
• knowing the shared values between and across different religions

Session 3:
In the last session, we appreciated the interaction of the three elements of the Interfaith Triangle as we examined the Art of Interfaith Leadership:
• Attitudes
• Knowledge
• Relationships

These three sessions presented the raw materials of interfaith cooperation. If we want a bridge of interfaith cooperation, we are the ones who are going to build it with these materials.

Now we hear from Eboo how we develop a community of bridge builders in the Art of Interfaith Leadership. In this session we learn the need to:
• Voice
• Act
• Engage

Play the entire DVD for Session 4.

VOICE

Inspiration from the Life of Martin Luther King Jr.
(transcribed from the DVD teaching of Eboo Patel)

This story comes toward the end of the 380 days of walking to work during the Montgomery bus boycott when King and his compatriots in Montgomery experienced the fire bombing of King's home, false arrests, being fired from work and harassment of all kinds. Someone asked King if winning the opportunity to sit front to back in the buses of one provincial city in the American South was worth all the hardship. Didn't he feel angry and didn't he want revenge against the men who made this so hard?

King *uses his voice* to say these words:

> *This is not the time for revenge. This is the time for redemption. This is the time for reconciliation. This is the time to build the beloved community. We have to go beyond the acrimony of the last year and get to creating a nation of black and white, of Gentile and Jew, of Protestant and Catholic together, that is a beloved community.*

> *Many people want to make of me many things, but at bottom I am the son of a Baptist minister and I am the grandson of a Baptist minister and my vocation, as the son of the living God and Jesus Christ, is the highest vocation and commitment that I have.*

Eboo notes two things:
- The clarity of King's identity as a Christian and how that identity inspired him to be who he was.
- The ability to articulate that identity in the most beautiful and inspiring language even at the hardest times to bring others into this movement of equal dignity for all people.

Here are examples of leadership through *voice* from the small group meeting with Eboo:

> *Ian* speaks of a time when he was in early high school and stayed with a Jewish friend when his parents went away. The weekend of his visit coincided with a Jewish holiday when Ian's friend's family was celebrating with their whole family. At the meal they started going around the table, reading prayers aloud. When it came to Ian, there was an anticipatory silence. Ian took the book and read the prayer. The mood changed because someone whom they knew had a limited background in Jewish faith was still willing to participate. Ian reflects that *hearing his voice* gave him a confidence in his relationship with his friend at that time that was important as they both got older and as their families came to know each other.

Nick talks about a time when he shifts his focus from Middle East studies to Islamic studies. There was one lecture when the professor was going over stories in the Qur'an that had parallels in Hebrew Scriptures and the New Testament. At one point the teacher asked Nick to stand up and share with the class the story from the Bible that paralleled the one from the Qur'an that they were reading. Nick did that. Ever since then, Nick's professor and classmates have turned to Nick to *hear his voice* in things that matter to them. That was what launched him into *bringing his voice into the discussion* where he was clearly in the minority.

1. When have you had the opportunity to use your voice as an interfaith leader?

2. If you haven't had that opportunity, who inspires you to take that risk?

3. Leadership is not just what we do personally. Yes, it begins with who we are, what we do, and what we model, but ultimately leadership is about how we get others to do these positive things: *to lift up their voices.* Recall a time when you encouraged another person to use their voice in the interest of interfaith cooperation and development.

4. Leadership is rooted in identity. Voice is an expression of that identity. When a person's voice is rooted in a clear sense of their identity you can hear that authority coming through in what they say and how they say it. Borrowing the phrasing of Martin Luther King Jr., speak to the members of the group about your own identity: *Many people want to make of me many things, but at bottom I am...*

5. After completing your statement, conclude with: *This is the highest vocation and commitment that I have.*

Inspiration from the Life of Martin Luther King Jr.
(transcribed from the DVD teaching of Eboo Patel)

In 1950, King was a student at Crozer Theological Seminary in Chester, Pennsylvania, when he went to hear a great African-American scholar and preacher, Mordecai Johnson, the President of Howard University, give a sermon on Christian love at Friendship House, Philadelphia. In that sermon, Mordecai Johnson uses as the embodiment of Christian love the figure of an Indian Hindu, Mahatma Gandhi.

I sometimes wonder what must have been going through the mind of young Martin Luther King Jr. He's 21 years old at the time, from Atlanta, where his dad is a Baptist minister. He grows up in a Baptist household, he goes to the Baptist Morehouse College, and he's at seminary learning the Protestant Christian tradition, and here he is going to hear this great African-American theologian and scholar speak on Christian love, and who does this guy talk about? A Hindu! There's a part of me that marvels at the fact that King didn't just get up, turn around and walk out of that hall. His entire life of being around the Christian tradition is turned upside down by the idea that the person who might have carried out Jesus' ethic of love and nonviolence best in the 20th Century is not a Christian.

Instead, what he does is *engage*. He *engages* the Hindu tradition and not in a way that he forfeits his own and questions the truth of his own; instead he feels more confident in his own tradition because he knows that the waters of nonviolence run through Christianity. He has read of those waters. He has been inspired by them. But he had a narrow interpretation of Christianity and nonviolence; he thought that non-violence and Christianity meant how you treated your neighbors and friends. It was a personal ethic. But here Gandhi is saying that nonviolence is a social reform ethic; it's a public ethic; it's the way that we ought to run movements and societies.

So King goes back to Crozer and he digs deep into Gandhi's work and deep into the Christian tradition and asks the question, "What is it in the Christian tradition that would give me a social reform ethic of nonviolence?" I have this image of King in the Crozer Theological Seminary library, a stack of Christian books on his left and the works of Hinduism, Gandhi and the Bhagavad gita on his right. And he's going back and forth between these two piles, *engaging* the Hindu tradition in a way that deepens and illumines his own.

Here are examples of leadership through *engagement* from the small group meeting with Eboo:

> *Maham* tells of a Muslim friend who fell in love with a Hindu woman. This was a kind of Romeo and Juliet story, but with a happy ending. It was possible to see the great divides between the families in spite of the love between the two young people that brought the families together. Maham took the initiative to *engage the situation* and to take the Hindu woman to the mosque to introduce her to the people there, including her soon-to-be family. Then she took the Muslim friend to the Hindu temple. She spoke of creating

situations where they would act together in preparations for their wedding. Maham came to see in this experience that the breakthroughs in interfaith relationship are not through great movements, but through these more personal and intimate actions and moments.

Vicki speaks of a time in grad school when there happened to be a very diverse religious group. The group members noticed that, although they all went to class together, they never talked about what they were experiencing from the perspective of their own religions. So, being good grad students, they got together and read papers to one another about their perspectives on particular issues like love and sacrifice from the point of view of their traditions. Most of them ended up teaching in seminaries with the advantage of this experience in seminary. It made them think differently about how they taught in their denominational settings. Vicki noticed that she became more attuned to colleagues "deriding" the practice of other religious institutions "across the street." As a result she made the choice to speak up. Vicki hopes that small interfaith groups meeting in this way, engaging with and encouraging one another, may go out into other parts of the religious world and take those kinds of initiative with them, like seeds.

1. What are times when you took the initiative to engage with another tradition or another person from another tradition?

2. How are you now engaging with opportunities presented in relationship to other traditions?

3. Leadership is not just what we do personally. Yes, it begins with who we are, what we do, and what we model, but ultimately leadership is about how we get others to do these positive things: *to engage in positive relationships.* How do you facilitate *engagement* between people of different religious backgrounds?

4. You will notice in the examples above from Eboo (about Martin Luther King), Maham and Vicki, that there is a high degree of self-awareness. For example:
   — the moment when MLK was suddenly confronted by a dramatic reversal in everything he had come to expect about the living of his faith, and decided to move ahead into a new way of being in relation to his faith
   — the moment when Maham realized that it was possible for these two young people who were in love to be accompanied beyond their own misgivings and the resistance of their families, and decided to engage on their behalf
   — the moment when Vicki became aware of the potential present in small interfaith groups, and decided to engage in situations where people of other faiths were being unjustly "derided"

5. Based on your experience, what qualities and skills does it take to facilitate healthy creative *engagement* in an interfaith situation? Which ones do you want to expand in your own being?

ACT

Inspiration from the Life of Martin Luther King Jr.
(transcribed from the DVD teaching of Eboo Patel)

King's first call is to the pulpit of Dexter Ave. Baptist Church in Montgomery. He thinks of himself as an intellectual preacher and gives these highfalutin sermons to the well-educated flock at Dexter Avenue Church. And then on a fateful day in 1955, Rosa Parks refuses to give up her seat on a bus, and the senior African-American leadership in Montgomery asks the question, "Who has the intellect, and the force and the outsider-enough status that's not involved in the internecine squabbles of Montgomery to be able to lead this new organization? *The Montgomery Improvement Association.*"

E. D. Nixon and Ralph Abernathy and others choose King, and King has the opportunity to do the third part of interfaith leadership which is to *act*. He pushes the African-American Christian community of Montgomery in the direction that he'd read about Gandhi going: the example of the Salt March. He said that the African-American community needed to boycott the buses in Montgomery, not ride them at all, not give them their money until they implemented the just laws of desegregation and the total integration of the buses. And until then they will walk to work and engage with each other arm-in-arm in this act of civil disobedience, nonviolently, with love. And that's precisely what King does.

He does this really powerful beautiful action that puts on display the dignity of this community, in injustices they've experienced, and their decision to respond to that injustice boldly but with love.

Here are examples of leadership through *acting* from the small group meeting with Eboo:

Gautam talks about the importance of *acting*, by speaking of a friend, Greg Damhorst, who initiated "A Million Meals for Haiti: Interfaith Action" on his campus. Greg was a student at University of Illinois, wondering what he could do in response to the disaster in Haiti. He ended up bringing together 5,000 students from a diversity of faith traditions and from no faith at all to serve the needs of the Haitian community. For Gautam it was life changing to see Greg's values translated into some real world action through the collaboration of so diverse a community.

Eboo notes that Greg and Gautam and the other students in "A Million Meals for Haiti" were not only acting themselves, they were also mobilizing other people. They committed themselves to action, modeled the action, and then encouraged others to do it together.

1. What are times when you *acted* as an interfaith leader in ways of which you are proud?

3. Leadership is not just what we do personally. Yes, it begins with who we are, what we do, and what we model, but ultimately leadership is about how we get others to do these positive things: *to act in ways that are bold as love*. What are times when you've initiated a powerful interaction in a relationship between two other people in an engaged moment to get them to act?

2. How are you taking action now?

4. How do you create situations where other people can take action?

5. Eboo tells a moving personal story of how he was summoned into interfaith leadership by a particular experience in high school.

In the high school I went to my best friends were a Nigerian Evangelical, a South Indian Hindu, a Cuban Jew, a Lutheran, a Mormon and a Catholic. We would talk about everything but religion. There were a couple of months during my high-school years when a group of thugs in the school started to go after my Jewish friend with anti-Semitic slurs and comments, and I watched the horror happen, and I did nothing.

A couple of years later my Jewish friend said to me, "How is it that you watched what I went through with this ugly derision of my sacred tradition and you did nothing?" It was the most humiliating moment of my life, listening to him say that. I talked to my dad about it, and my dad was so disappointed. He said, "You failed your friend, but you also failed your faith, because Islam calls you to stand up for those who are hurting especially when they're from a different tradition. You have a special responsibility to those who are not Muslim, who are not part of your community, who are experiencing pain. I thought to myself, "I'm never going to be that guy again."

So, I'm involved in leadership because I didn't want to fail my friends or my faith again. We have to recognize that the territory is not neutral. The winds of prejudice and conflict and tension are blowing, and there are people who are building barriers and bombs of religion. If I'm not building a bridge, I just forfeit the territory to them. That's where I started.

I think that leaders ought to be measured by the people who are part of their movement. Don't measure the quality of my voice by what I say; measure it by Caryn, Maham, Nick, Gautam and Ian, and the community that we are building around the interfaith movement—the quality of the voices of other people—the quality of their action—the depth of their engagement. Leadership is about nurturing movements.

What are the stories from your life that compel you to act in the name of justice and against prejudice, in the name of freedom and against oppression, in the name of pluralism and against bigotry?

IF YOU ARE A GROUP OF DIVERSE RELIGIOUS BACKGROUND...

1. Share with one another the stories from your history and tradition that inspire you in the art of interfaith leadership.

2. What personal experiences have moved you to commit some of the energy, skills and passion of your life to this movement of interfaith collaboration?

3. What are the most important aspects of your religious identity? You might use this stem in sharing: *These are the things from my tradition that form the firm ground on which I confidently stand...*

Following the session you will continue to think about issues raised both on the DVD and in your small group. This suggestion for journaling is offered to support you in continuing your reflection beyond the session time.

Continue to reflect on the ways that your *leadership* is rooted in *identity*. You might not have had time to work with this reflective framework in the session. It lends itself to ongoing journal writing. Borrowing the phrasing of Martin Luther King Jr., think further on the aspects of identity that are foundational to your highest vocation and commitment:

> *Many people want to make of me many things, but at bottom I am…*

Conclude your statement with:

> *This is the highest vocation and commitment that I have.*

CLOSING

From the Jewish tradition comes the *Birkat Kohanim*, the Priestly Blessing, which we find in Numbers 6:24-26. This is also part of the blessing that many Jews say over children every Friday night as part of Sabbath celebration. These verses of the Priestly Blessing are among the oldest in continuous liturgical use:

> The Lord bless you and keep you;
> the Lord make his face to shine upon you, and be gracious to you;
> the Lord lift up his countenance upon you, and give you peace.

In the Christian tradition we find the Prayer of Saint Francis of Assisi:

> Lord, make me an instrument of your peace.
> Where there is hatred, let me sow love;
> where there is injury, pardon;
> where there is doubt, faith;
> where there is despair, hope;
> where there is darkness, light;
> and where there is sadness, joy.
>
> O Divine Master, grant that I may not so much seek
> to be consoled as to console;
> to be understood as to understand;
> to be loved as to love.
> For it is in giving that we receive;
> it is in pardoning that we are pardoned;
> and it is in dying that we are born to eternal life. *Amen.*

SESSION | 5

THE ROLE OF COLLEGES, SEMINARIES AND HOUSES OF WORSHIP

BEFORE THE SESSION

Many participants like to come to the group conversation after considering individually some of the issues that will be raised. The following five reflective activities are intended to open your minds, memories and emotions regarding some aspects of this session's topic. Use the space provided here to note your reflections.

1. Visit your closest seminary and talk with people who know about the curriculum and about the encouragement of interfaith relationships. Take with you the section below "Challenges for Seminaries" (pp. 80-81) as a guide to some of the issues you could ask about at the seminary.

2. Is there a faith community in your town or city where there seems to be a lot going on in terms of interfaith programming and relationship? Make an appointment to talk to someone there about their commitment to interfaith cooperation, their strategies for pursuing that priority, and the surprises they have experienced along the way.

3. Turn to section III of this session: "Jesus' Theology of Interfaith Cooperation" (pp. 87-89). Take time to read the story of the Good Samaritan and Eboo Patel's reflections following it. Come to the session prepared to engage in the conversation about the passage, the issues raised by Eboo and your own insights.

4. In the "Group Life" section at the end of this session (p. 91), you will find 7 stems to complete as part of an evaluation and feedback process for the whole series. Do some reflection on those 7 points prior to the session.

5. How have you changed as a result of your participation in this series? With change comes new opportunities and interests. What are you now ready for that you might not have been able to consider prior to your participating in this series?

This is the final meeting of the group. Rather than thinking about building your learning community, you are naturally thinking about ending it and reflecting with gratitude on what it has meant for you all to be together in these five sessions. There are several places in the session where you will be encouraged to think into the future, beyond this series. At the end of the session you will find reflective questions for you to consider as part of your evaluation and closing.

 Play the DVD for Session 5, just over 30 minutes.

CHALLENGES ENOUGH FOR EVERYONE

The comments on the DVD address all players in church life: seminary teachers, pastors-in-training, congregational ministers and leaders, members of faith communities. There are realities and challenges enough for everyone in this rapidly changing area of religious life.

Take time with the three areas of challenge that follow. Where you feel confident to develop proposals as a group, do so, *using the space provided to write in your strategies for creative change.*

CHALLENGES FOR CONGREGATIONS

1. We feel the call to make the realm of God visible here so that God's goodness is truly expressed in compassion and justice. How can we do that while recognizing that there are diverse groups of people here in this community living many expressions of faith? What does it mean for us to be neighbors here? How will we work alongside our neighbors from other traditions?

2. What resources (like Eboo Patel's book, *Sacred Ground* and this study, *Embracing Interfaith Cooperation*) will support and direct the development of interfaith literacy and leadership in congregations?

3. Interfaith interaction is going to happen. How can we be on the side of the positive?

Vicki, one of the group members meeting with Eboo, issues this challenge to congregations:

We live in increasingly diverse neighborhoods, but a lot of the time we don't see what's right there in front of our eyes because we're not expecting to see that, in fact, we do have neighbors who have very different perspectives on the spiritual life and on God. But here's the thing: a lot of local religious communities know that, whatever is at the center of their faith, their faith calls them to go out from where they are and be engaged in the world.

We all want to do good in the world, but we're little congregations. Well, who's across the street? Who else might want to do some good? There are all kinds of possibilities; it's not rocket science! Let's open our eyes. Being willing to step outside our red doors takes an act of courage, but the rewards are terrific.

4. Our proposals for shaping the life of our congregation in interfaith awareness and cooperation:

CHALLENGES FOR SEMINARIES

1. Together review and respond to these eight challenges that Eboo and Nick formulate for seminaries:

   - Around the country I've noticed that people are able to talk about theology and racial reconciliation, theology and the environment, theology and poverty, but when I ask about the theology of interfaith cooperation, there's silence. It's not a muscle that's been exercised yet.

   - Just as people take Greek, Hebrew and New Testament studies in seminaries, there will have to be a similar emphasis on the theology of interfaith cooperation in seminaries.

   - If we are going to have interfaith literacy in America and the world, especially if we are going to have theologies of interfaith cooperation, the fountainhead for that knowledge base is going to be seminaries.

   - What resources (like Eboo Patel's book, *Sacred Ground*) need to be available to support and direct the development of interfaith literacy and leadership in the seminary?

- Clearly, a theology of interfaith cooperation is there in bits and pieces, but seminaries are going to have to stitch the parts into a whole.

- College campuses, with which seminaries can have a special relationship, are unique places in our society that lift up people's particular identities, so you have all kinds of groups: Hindu, Muslim, Jewish, Evangelical, Catholic and secular, to mention a few. These groups are well respected and resourced. College campuses believe in bridges between different groups; they believe that students ought to build those bridges; they believe in civic engagement and social action volunteerism. They are places where all that social capital is concentrated in five to ten square blocks. There are few places in the world where you can go from a vague notion to actual action faster than on a college campus.

- How do we actually help up-and-coming ministers to think about what it is from our faith tradition that inspires us to engage in interfaith cooperation?

- How do we encourage teachers and students in seminary to develop relationships with people of other faith traditions as an expectation, not just an option?

2. Our proposals for deepening the life and work of seminaries in interfaith awareness and cooperation:

1. Together review and respond to these very challenging questions faced by pastors, ministers, priests and lay leaders:

   - What do I think about the fact that there are other religions out there that may or may not be in line with the theology and practice of my own faith tradition?

   - Beyond the theology of religious differences, what is my theology of interfaith?

   - How do I stay faithful to my theological system while wrestling with other theological systems?

   - My congregation is located in a very culturally diverse community. What is the way that I can go about making the realm of God visible here so that God's goodness is truly expressed in compassion and justice?

- If you are an ordained leader in a Christian church and a mosque in your neighborhood gets burned to the ground or damaged in some way, what do you tell your congregants? How do you inspire members of your faith community to reach out and care for their neighbors?

- If members of my congregation come to me as their pastor to gather information about other faiths, I always encourage them to go ask the members of other faiths who are right there in our neighborhood.

- How will you create spaces where the members of your faith community can gather and interact with people of other faith communities to meet and to talk?

2. Our proposals for enabling church leaders to act courageously and competently in such a time:

1. Review and respond as Eboo and Nick speak passionately about their shared vision of interfaith cooperation:

   • Interfaith cooperation has to become a social norm in America.

   • If we're going to move interfaith cooperation into our civic fabric, there has to be a neighborhood dimension to it as well.

   • Even if you're not connected immediately to a house of worship or a seminary or a college campus, it's likely that someone in your immediate circle is, and that's somebody you could influence.

• We have this dream at Interfaith Youth Core that one day every major city in America will have a day of interfaith service, just like there is a breast cancer walk or marathon.

• In whatever way you're involved in your neighborhood and city, you can think about how to be an interfaith leader and apply your voice and engage to act in that setting.

• Even people who call themselves atheist or agnostic, should feel welcomed into this discourse.

- As an American in a diverse society is it not a part of my civic duty to be curious about the person sitting next to me—my fellow American—to engage and learn from their story?

- If you're ever tempted to be drawn into negative thoughts about interfaith relationship, then remember these sessions when two Muslims, a Jew, two Episcopalians, one Evangelical, and someone with a Hindu-Jain background came together for connection, inspiration and enrichment.

- Am I pausing long enough to say to the person I see engaged in religious practice, "Tell me, why is that important to you? Tell me about the role that plays in your background."

2. These are visions and challenges. Which ones do you feel ready to pick up as you come to the conclusion of this resource, *Embracing Interfaith Cooperation?*

- It's so easy to look at the evening news and believe that religious diversity is simply a recipe for conflict.

3. What plans do you have personally to extend the learning of this time into engagement and action?

4. What plans do you have to do that as a group?

JESUS' THEOLOGY OF INTERFAITH COOPERATION

Several times Eboo Patel makes reference to the gospel story of The Good Samaritan as a foundation for Jesus' teaching about interfaith cooperation. Although a familiar story to most Christians, it may not have been explored as a source of instruction and requirement in the matter of interfaith relationship.

1. Read the story, printed here, being open to the insights it has to offer people of the Way of Jesus concerning relationship with people of other faiths.

Luke 10:25-37
The Parable of the Good Samaritan

Just then a lawyer stood up to test Jesus. "Teacher," he said, "what must I do to inherit eternal life?" He said to him, "What is written in the law? What do you read there?" He answered, "You shall love the Lord your God with all your heart, and with all your soul, and with all your strength, and with all your mind; and your neighbor as yourself."' And he said to him, "You have given the right answer; do this, and you will live."

But wanting to justify himself, he asked Jesus, "And who is my neighbor?" Jesus replied, "A man was going down from Jerusalem to Jericho, and fell into the hands of robbers, who stripped him, beat him, and went away, leaving him half dead. Now by chance a priest was going down that road; and when he saw him, he passed by on the other side. So likewise a Levite, when he came to the place and saw him, passed by

on the other side. But a Samaritan* while travelling came near him; and when he saw him, he was moved with pity. He went to him and bandaged his wounds, having poured oil and wine on them. Then he put him on his own animal, brought him to an inn, and took care of him. The next day he took out two denarii, gave them to the innkeeper, and said, "Take care of him; and when I come back, I will repay you whatever more you spend." Which of these three, do you think, was a neighbor to the man who fell into the hands of the robbers?" He said, "The one who showed him mercy." Jesus said to him, "Go and do likewise."

*A word about Samaritans:
- The Samaritans were residents of the district of Samaria who lived in villages around Mt. Gerizim.
- The Jews and Samaritans had a common heritage but differed from one another with regard to the relative sanctity of Jerusalem and Mt. Gerizim.
- Jews regarded the Samaritans as a people foreign to themselves, in spite of having a shared heritage.
- They avoided contact with one another partly because of the difference in legal traditions regarding the cleanliness of vessels.
- On one occasion the adversaries of Jesus refer to him contemptuously as "a Samaritan."
- The itinerary of Jesus in Mark seems to reflect a standard Jewish practice of avoiding Samaria in pilgrimages to Jerusalem.

- Not all the residents of Samaria were members of this Samaritan community. There were people of several cultural backgrounds living in the area.
- As a religious sect, the Samaritans are a strict, Torah-observing party with a pride in their religious heritage. They saw themselves and not the Jews as the bearers of the true faith of ancient Israel.

—Source: *Harper's Bible Dictionary* (HarperSanFrancisco, 1985, pp. 898-899)

2. Now read this excerpt from Eboo Patel's book, *Sacred Ground, Pluralism, Prejudice, and the Promise of America* (Boston, MA: Beacon Press, 2012), in which he reflects on this well-known story from Christian scriptures:

> *I imagine Jesus telling this parable about a man from the other community, the despised community, to a large gathering of his main audience—Jews. As Jesus proceeds, describing the brutal robbery, the two men who see and ignore the traveler, and finally the Samaritan who nurses him back to health, I imagine the series of realizations, the layers of understanding, occurring in the minds of this audience.*

> *Clearly, helping those in need is an important part of this story. Well, why don't the priest and the Levite—both representing important positions in the community of Jew—stop to help? They were both aware of the law. In fact, they were expert in the law, and had responsibility for interpreting and implementing it. Perhaps it was their very expertise that prevented them from helping. One of the laws forbade the touching of the dead; another forbade them from touching*

> *Gentiles. Perhaps the priest and the Levite feared that the man was dead, or thought he was a Gentile, and chose to follow the letter of the law so that they would not become unclean. Clearly, Jesus is saying there is a good higher than following the letter of the law—the ethic of helping one in need.*

> *But if that were indeed the main point of the story, why not have the priest or the Levite choose to override the letter of the law in the spirit of the higher good? Certainly, that would have brought home the holiness of helping. Something else is happening here.*

> *The priest and the Levite get only three short sentences in the story. The scripture is not about them. The man who is hurt is also barely described at all. It is the Samaritan who gets all the attention. His actions are described in rich detail—using oil and wine (valuable resources) to dress the wounds, using his own animal to transport the man, spending his own time caring for him, offering the innkeeper whatever money is necessary to nurse him back to health.*

> *Jesus is telling a story about people who were not a part of his audience. In fact, he is making one the hero of his story. The Samaritans who were not just "other," and not just despised; they were heretic, people of a different path.*

> *When Jesus finishes, he turns to the man who asked "Who is my neighbor?" and gently suggests he answer the question based on the story he just heard. The lawyer is unable to bring himself to speak of the man the way Jesus does, to say the word Samaritan. But he gets the point of the story: "He who showed mercy on him," he tells the teacher. Jesus doesn't force him further.*

Embracing Interfaith Cooperation   88   Session 5: The Role of Colleges, Seminaries and Houses of Worship

He trusts the moral will work its way through the man's prejudices. The story ends with Jesus telling the lawyer, and the crowd that has gathered, "Go and do likewise."

I imagine the question lingering, the stillness in the air, the sense of joy and fear and desire that this story has provoked in the audience. I imagine them nervously looking around at one another. No heretics here. No despised ones around. No "others" present. The Samaritans are safely elsewhere. I imagine the comfort this community felt being amid their own as the story opened. And then slowly, as the story develops, as the characters are introduced and the action unfolds, a nagging feeling starts to set in. The respected leaders among them—the priest and the Levite—are not the heroes of this story. Elsewhere in the Bible, Jesus makes it clear that he disagrees with the theology of the Samaritans (John 4:1-27). Still, it is the Samaritan, the heretic, Jesus tells them to emulate. Jesus seems to be saying it is not enough to stay within the fold of the faithful, not enough even to follow the way, the truth and the life. To attain the eternal, the story suggests, you have to engage with people who believe differently than you.

In your group, reflect about the meaning of Jesus' parable in this interfaith context.

IF YOU ARE A GROUP OF DIVERSE RELIGIOUS BACKGROUND...

1. You have come to the end of this small group experience. What do you need to say to one another as part of your closing?

2. Name the gifts that each member of the group has brought to this experience.

3. In what ways do you intend to extend this experience of interfaith relationship into the future?

These are topics for evaluation and reflection that can facilitate the closing of a group, enabling the members to feel finished with the experience, and free to move on to the next place of learning and engagement:

1. Things I really liked about this learning experience…

2. Things we could have done better in the interest of our learning…

3. Things I learned that will make a difference at this time in my life…

4. Some very positive outcomes for our group members…

5. Messages we have for our church about how to build on this experience…

6. Resources we encourage our church to have on hand in the interests of interfaith awareness…

7. Other unfinished business…

Following the session, you will continue to think about issues raised both on the DVD and in your small group. This suggestion is offered to support you in continuing your personal reflection beyond the session time.

This session has raised the issue of a theology of interfaith cooperation. How has your participation in this series of five sessions shaped your theology: the way you know God; the way you see religion; the place that the great spiritual leaders and prophets, like Jesus, Buddha, Muhammad and Moses, hold in your faith journey?

CLOSING

At the end of the session, seven of the members of the group offer blessings from their own tradition. Those are offered here—as a blessing for you—in their uniqueness and in their connectedness:

Love the Lord, your God
with all your heart, soul, mind and strength
and love your neighbor as yourself.

***

May you always have the strength and courage
to see and to face the reality of things.

***

Serve everyone and everything
without discrimination, without condition.
Just love unconditionally.

***

May God give you goodness.

***

Bread for your journey.

***

Be not afraid.

***

Shalom.

Printed in the USA
CPSIA information can be obtained
at www.ICGtesting.com
JSHW051347310724
67297JS00003B/10

9 781606 741191